Close Your Eyes So You Can See Me

Close Your Eyes So You Can See Me

John B. Reid

CLOSE YOUR EYES SO YOU CAN SEE ME

John B. Reid

ISBN 1537422456

ISBN 13: 9781537422459

This book is dedicated to all of my fellow travelers on the road to happy destiny. And to my wife Gaby, who has endured much in our journey together. You are the love of my life. I also wish to include in this dedication my son, Jonathan, who is the very rising and setting of the Sun in my life.

I would be remiss if I did not acknowledge my dear friend and Archbishop H.E. Donald L. Jolly-Gabriel, Ph.D. of the Western Rite Syriac Orthodox Church of Antioch North America Diocese, who has stood by my side in good times and bad, always serving as a beacon of God's light in my life. May we remain steadfast in our search for spiritual Truth.

Contents

Introduction   ix

Chapter One   Change Your Thinking, Change
                        Your Life   1

Chapter Two   Let Not Your Heart Be Troubled   7

Chapter Three   You Can Be a Winner   10

Chapter Four   Let Go and Let God   21

Chapter Five   Finding a God of Your Own
                        Understanding   26

Chapter Six   An Inside Job   31

Chapter Seven   What Is Hell? What Is Heaven?   36

Chapter Eight   Race Consciousness   42

Chapter Nine   The Greatest of These Is Love   46

Chapter Ten   Affirmative Prayer   51

Chapter Eleven   Resentment, a Cancer to the Soul   58

Chapter Twelve   The Beatitudes Long Form   63

Chapter Thirteen   No Man Can Serve Two Masters   68

Chapter Fourteen   Living in Today   75

Chapter Fifteen   God, Love, and Marriage   79

Chapter Sixteen   By Your Actions, Not Your Words   86

Chapter Seventeen   The Prodigal Son   94

Introduction

Every person must come to a point in their life when they ask themselves, "What do I really believe about God, and what is meant by 'right relationship' with Him?" We also ask ourselves, "Does God really hear and act upon my prayers, or am I fooling myself?"

The purpose of this book is to discuss these questions and many more. This book is not being presented simply from the point of view of a "book on Theology," but rather, from an experiential standpoint. In other words, this is not a book written to fit into one particular religion or denomination, but an all-inclusive approach, trying to get out from under the position of "who is right," and trying to move toward "what is right."

In this book I hope to come out from behind the altar, so to speak, and have a meaningful conversation with you, my brothers and sisters, as a beloved member of our Father's loving family. This means that I shall share in this book some of my own personal experiences, dreams, pains, learning and life changes.

It is my hope that in reading this book you will over-come some of your fears in asking questions about God. I hope you will do more than just read this book and say to yourself, "He's a priest, so his way of viewing things must be the absolute way of seeing things." Take time to think for yourself about the ideas in this book. Ask yourself how the propositions set forth in this book fit into your own belief system. The purpose of reading any book on spirituality should be to use the information to shape and form your own spiritual path leading to God, and then to take this new information and share it with others in order to help them ask questions and grow.

A wise man once said, "When one person raises his consciousness by any degree, he raises the consciousness of the entire world with him."

May God's blessings and favor be upon you always.

Chapter One

Change Your Thinking, Change Your Life

It has been said by many wise men and women throughout the ages, "To have more, you must become more in your consciousness." These words ring true. If you want more good in your life you must make room for it. In other words, to receive more good into your living experience you need to create more space in your consciousness for the good that you desire. But how does one do this?

To make room for the new you must get rid of the old. Jesus said, "No one sews a patch of unshrunk cloth on an old garment, for the patch will pull away from the garment, making the tear worse. Neither do men pour new wine into old wineskins. If they do, the skins will burst, the wine will run out and the wineskins will be ruined. No, they pour new wine into new wineskins, and both are preserved" (Matthew 9:16, 17 NIV).

To have more in your life, whether it is money, love, peace, joy of faith, you must change your old shame-based belief systems. Which belief systems? The ones that say to you on a daily basis that you do not deserve to have good things in your life. This belief must change if you are to live up to your highest potential.

Another belief that has to go is the age-old message that has been passed down from generation to generation, which says there is nobility in suffering. Let me take this opportunity to state that God did not put you here to suffer. The Father described by Jesus would not do such a thing. If He would, we could not call Him a loving Father. Let me give you Jesus' words on this matter. "Which of you, if his son asks for bread, will give him a stone? Or if he asks for a fish, will give him a snake? If you, though you are evil, know to give good gifts to your children, how much more will your Father in heaven give good gifts to those who ask Him!" (Matthew 7:9, 10, 11). I want to be clear on this point. God loves you and His will for you is one of love, joy, peace and prosperity. However, He never interferes with our free will. Suffering comes from the thoughts we hold in consciousness and not from God's will.

You may be asking yourself right now, "If God does not want for me to suffer, then why do I have so much turmoil in my life? Where does it all come from?" Suffering comes from wrong use of Divine Laws. Divine Law states that all thought is creative. **All** thoughts are creative, not just the thoughts that bring about the things we desire to have in our life. This is why you must change your thinking in order to change your life, Don't be afraid to change your mind about things.

I invite you to start changing your life by changing just a few of the ways you view life. In the morning begin your day by saying, "I thank God that this day my life is filled with love, peace and joy. I open my mind to new possibilities, knowing that there are many avenues, but one source from which my good comes to me." During your lunch break say, "I rejoice for I know that God wants only good for me in my life and I accept that good here and now." When retiring at night say, "I thank God for the gifts in my life. I am grateful for new insights that lead me to greater fulfillment in my living experience." Do this for thirty days with an open mind and with the willingness to change.

As you say these affirmations each day, do not look for outward changes at first. The reason I say this is because every thought you hold in consciousness is creative. If you are continually looking for something that you think will not be there, that will be what you manifest in your experience, nothing. Jesus tells us, "Truly I say to you, whoever should say to this mountain, be moved and fall into the sea, and does not doubt in his heart, but believes that what he says is done, it will be done to him. Therefore I say to you, anything you pray for and ask, believe that you will receive it, and it will be done for you" (Mark 11:23, 24 Lamsa Translation). It's an inside job! If you want to change what's happening on the outside, you must first change what is happening on the inside.

If you want to experience more in your life you must get past the idea that there is not enough good to go around. We live in an abundant universe, which is willing to supply us with the things we need. But, it can only do for us, through us. We must clear the path in our consciousness, be truly willing to accept all the good that the universe has to offer, and be ready to take action. We must be willing to do the footwork in creating more abundance in our living experience. Faith without works is dead. Our problem lies strictly in our consciousness and not in the willingness of the universe. So get ready to change your B.S. (Belief Systems).

By having more in your life you are not depriving anyone of anything. There is more than enough good in this universe to go around. It is important to the world around you that you demonstrate prosperity in your life. When you make this demonstration you can help others to realize that they are capable of having more in their life as well. In fact, it is a Divine Law that if you want to live a life filled with love, peace, joy, and abundance, you have to give it away in order to keep it. This is what some call the Divine Paradox. It has been my experience, as well as the experience of many others, that you cannot live your life in selfishness and have a steady flow of love, peace, joy, health and prosperity. Why not? Because these thoughts are part of the belief system that says there is not enough good to go around. Henceforth, according to your thought held in consciousness you will demonstrate the like manifestation.

In keeping with this theory, if you go through life doing for others what they need to have done for free and for fun, you will manifest in your life more good than you could have ever imagined. To make this point I would like to share with you the wisdom of a friend of mine who taught me this principle. My friend, Chuck Chamberlain, went through a time in his life when he had no money coming in. After he underwent a spiritual experience, which changed his whole way of living, he discovered that he was a millionaire. Chuck did not set out to get rich; his prosperity was the result of him giving freely of everything he had. I can remember talking with Chuck one time when somebody asked him, "Chuck, how long do I have to practice these principles before I get as much money as you have?" Chuck just laughed and said, "Let me tell you something. I went out to help God's kids do what they needed to have done because I wanted to, and when I wasn't looking God snuck up on me and made me a rich man."

All the time I knew Chuck he was looking to see what he could do for somebody else. He was perhaps the happiest and most spiritually centered person I have ever met.

When Chuck died he knew he was simply returning to his Heavenly Father. Chuck was one of the most loving people this world has ever known. I can remember him saying to me one time,

"If you don't remember anything else I say to you, just remember that I love you and everything will be all right."

I share this with you in order to show you that what I have written in this book is more than theory; this way of life really works. This is Truth in its highest form. I have seen it over and over again with my own eyes. I have watched people go from desperation to joyful and prosperous living. I have seen people live in hell and then rise to heaven. In each case, when they changed their way of thinking their entire lives changed accordingly. In every case they had to go back and review their old beliefs about life and the world they lived in, and one by one they had to change their belief. They had to change their view. In other words, they had to stop looking "without" and start looking "within." In doing this they made a great discovery, they found that what they were looking for, they were looking with.

Notes

Chapter Two

Let Not Your Heart Be Troubled

In the fourteenth chapter of the Gospel of John, Jesus said, "Let not your heart be troubled; believe in God, and believe in me also. In my Father's house are many rooms; if it were not so, I would have told you. I go to prepare a place for you. And if I go and prepare a place for you, I will come again and take you to me that where I am you may be also. You know where I am going and you know the way" (John 14:1-4 Lamsa Translation).

Our relationship with God is to be based on love and not riddled with fear. Ergo, Jesus tells us, "Let not your heart be troubled." In trusting our Heavenly Father we should walk without fear, for He is always with us. The way has already been prepared, so we know that we are not on a path that leads to nowhere. We are on a path that leads us back home to the Father.

I would like to take these verses apart a little in order to shed some light on what they would mean if we used the idioms of Aramaic, which is the language Jesus spoke. With the idioms of the time, language and culture of Jesus I would translate the first verse like this: Let not your heart be filled with doubt. You have seen me and you believe in the Laws of God, believe as well in the truth of the spiritual Principles and Laws, which I have taught you.

The second verse I would translate: in the ways of my Father there is no lack. If it were not filled with perfect supply, with enough for all, I would have told you. I prepare the way for you through my teachings, which is now manifested. Verse three would continue: and in the demonstration of my truth, my teaching shall live in you so that the things I know, you shall know also.

The fourth verse should be expanded to say: and where I go (the spiritual plain) and the way or path (it should be noted that the only path to God is love) I have already taught you.

When we apply the idioms of the language that Jesus spoke we get deeper understanding of what He was trying to teach us. God is not a God of insufficiency. It is not God's desire that we should be impoverished. God has placed on earth everything we could possibly need to live in love, peace and joy. The gift from God was made in the foundation of the earth. He has given to us, as His people, all that we need. However, in order to make use of all the supply, which God has put here for us to use, we have to work together. It is part of the Divine Law that we are to feed one another. In practicing the principles taught by Jesus we are to be ambassadors of love. Until we do this, there will be hunger in the world. Not because there is not enough supply to feed the world, but rather, world hunger is caused by a worldly belief that says, "If I share with everyone there will be less for me and they will hold the same power as I do now." This way of thinking is not acceptable in the kingdom of God. This level of consciousness is the opposite of what Jesus taught.

Start today the seeds of love by being your brother's keeper and let not your heart be afraid, for you will know the true source of your good and you will truly be prosperous.

Notes

Chapter Three

You Can Be a Winner

I knew a man, who we will call Byron, who was raised in a home that was filled with rage and violence, as well as, physical and emotional abuse.

Byron was the youngest of four children being raised in a single parent home. Each of his siblings experienced much of the same abuse as did Byron. However, one of them, the brother who was two years older than Byron, chose to take out his frustrations on Byron by physically beating him just as their mother was doing to all of them.

Byron's mother was a chronic alcoholic who also suffered from Borderline Personality Disorder, and was Bi-polar (Manic/Depressive) with psychotic features. It was not uncommon for Byron's mother to put booze in the babies' bottles when putting the children down for the night. Even so, getting a full night of sleep in this house was rare for the children.

As Byron's mother would drink herself into a stupor, she would go around the house waking the children by slapping them, pulling them out of bed by their hair and yelling at them. Oftentimes, after everyone was awake, Byron's mother would announce that she was going to kill herself and she would tell the children that it was their fault. She would tell the children that they were ugly, stupid and unlovable, and that she could have a wonderful life if it were not for them. She would tell the children how much she hated them. This took place on almost a daily basis. On many occasions the local police and fire departments would respond to Byron's home because his mother had overdosed herself while drinking alcohol and taking various drugs.

As Byron grew older the abuse increased. One of the events that would recur on a regular basis was that Byron's mother, who was an atheist, would take all of the children to church on Sunday morning, then on the way home she would beat on the children and yell at them, "If there is a God, why doesn't He stop me from beating you? See, there is no God."

By the age of nine Byron was drinking alcohol on his own as often as he could get ahold of it. When he drank he felt equal to everyone around him. He liked how he felt when he drank because when he was sober he felt like he was ugly, stupid and unlovable just like his mother told him he was. He knew in his mind that everybody else was smarter than he was and he knew that he did not belong. He felt this way everywhere he went.

By age fourteen, Byron was a full-blown alcoholic and he knew the booze was killing him. He had to find a way out. In March of 1979 Byron became involved with a "twelve-step" program for alcoholics. Upon discovering that Byron had become involved with the twelve-step program, Byron's mother threw him out of her house, informing him that he was no longer welcome in her home. But Byron had found something in those meetings he had been attending, something he had sought after all of his life. In the twelve-step meetings he was introduced to a loving God and a group of loving people who shared with him their "experience, strength, and hope" in the light of their own recovery from a seemingly hopeless state of mind and body, being their alcoholism. Byron decided that it did not matter whether or not he lived on the street, he had found something he had to have, and that was recovery through a spiritual way of life.

Through most of his adolescent years Byron lived on the streets of his hometown. From time to time he would stay at his mother's house for a couple of weeks, only to be kicked out over and over again. Byron put himself through high school, spending many a night sleeping on the campus of his school.

One summer Byron spent six weeks in Juvenile Hall because somebody confronted Byron's mother about him living on the streets. Byron's mother dealt with the confrontation by calling the local police department and reporting Byron as a runaway, even though she Was the one who had put him out of her home.

Through all the insanity, with God's help, Byron stayed sober. After graduating high school, Byron began attending college. He had a goal in his heart to become a minister. School was not easy for Byron because he suffered from dyslexia. However, his sponsor in the twelve-step program reminded him on a regular basis, "You can quit tomorrow, but you will go today." With these words of wisdom, Byron never gave up. He also found strength in the Bible. One of the most powerful teachings from the Bible that kept him going was, "For men this is impossible, but for God everything is possible" (Matthew 19:26 Lamsa Translation).

As I write this book, Byron has been sober for more than twenty-four years and he is still very much involved with the twelve-step program, which brought him to recovery and to God. He knows that in order to maintain his own sobriety he must always be looking to see what he can do for somebody else suffering from the disease of alcoholism. As they say it in that particular program, "In order to keep it (sobriety), you must give it away."

Byron has obtained his goal of entering the ministry. Currently, he is serving as a priest with the Eastern Orthodox Church. He not only obtained a Master of Arts degree in religion, he received his Doctor of Philosophy in religion as well.

Byron is not bitter regarding his childhood and the abuse he underwent. He feels that his experience has helped him to be a good priest. He says, "When someone comes to you in pain, it's one thing to care, it's a whole other world to understand. It is because I understand that I do care."

The point I am trying to make is this; everybody has his or her own form of pain in life. We have choices as to what we will do with that discomfort. We can go through life complaining about our problems or we can make use of these troubles and experiences by walking through the problems and finding solutions that will help ourselves and others to become winners in life. Consider the oyster. When an oyster gets a grain of sand inside of it, the sand becomes an irritation. But after some time if the oyster doesn't simply discard or reject the grain of sand as though it had no value because it is uncomfortable for a time, the grain of sand transforms into a priceless pearl. I can remember a time in my own life when I was in a great deal of emotional pain due to a relationship in my life. A trusted friend gave me a wonderful piece of advice that I have used to this day. They said to me, "John, complete the experience, bless it and go on. But before you leave, make sure you have done everything you need to do in order to complete your experience in the situation because until you learn your lesson from the experience, you must re-experience the lesson. And when history repeats itself the price goes up."

We are given many opportunities to grow in life and to use the challenges we experience to increase our faith and to come into conscious unity with God. But in working through our pain we must come to see that the answer is not in the problem, the problem is in the problem. The answer is in the answer. Let me explain: as long as Byron kept his focus on the pain and cruelty of his childhood he remained stuck in the headache and sorrow of the situation; he could not see past the problem. But when he went in search of what he could do for others out of the motivation of love, he was able to use his experience to help and to heal other people, he himself received a healing as the result of loving others.

God is always willing to heal your life, but first you must admit you are in need of healing and then be willing to surrender everything, including your will and your life over to the care and keeping of our loving Father in heaven. I would like to remind you that God does not force His healing unto anyone, He is a gentleman. God does not interfere with our free will; He will allow you to hold onto your problems just as long as you want to hold onto them. He gives you complete freedom to make what you will of your life.

Of himself, "Byron did not have the power to solve his problem, so he found the Power that could, and that Power was God. With God directing the course of Byron's life, he now had the power to live sober and successfully. In order to make use of the power he found in God, he first had to admit that he, himself, was powerless over his problems and that his life was unmanageable by his will power. Jesus said it like this, "I do nothing of my own accord; But as my Father has taught me" (John 8:28 Lamsa Translation). Byron decided he needed new management in his life and the new manager would be God. As he did this, Byron also began following the suggestions of those people in the twelve-step program who had already found solutions to their living problems. It has been said by a person, "When the student is ready, the teacher will appear."

Jesus said, "I can do nothing of myself (John 5:30 Lamsa Translation). Jesus gave us the answer we have been looking for when He made this statement. It is not by our own power that our problems are solved, but by God's unlimited power. Jesus said, "With men this is impossible, but with God all things are possible" (Matthew 19:26 NIV). There is a slogan used by the people in Alcoholics Anonymous, which I find to be profound. They say, "Surrender to win." When we completely surrender our will and our lives, including all of the problems, into the care and keeping of God, and adopt an "attitude of gratitude," we discover that we are now living in the solution.

You, too, can be a winner if you stop trying to run your life through the limited power of self-will. Instead, power up with the power of God. Admit your faults honestly and be willing to start a new life. Accept God's love for you and allow others to love you until you learn to love yourself. Most importantly, the mark of a true winner is when you begin to share the answers you have found with other people who are trying to find their way down life's road. This is when you will truly discover what it is to know love.

Jesus spent His time here on earth loving people and being of service. Love and service were so important to Jesus that He told His disciples, "Let him who is great among you be the least, and he who is the leader be like the one who serves" (Luke 22:26 Lamsa Translation). "If anyone wants to be first, he must be the very last, and the servant of all" (Mark 9:35 NTV). Jesus taught His disciples how to be winners.

I would like you to consider for a moment the lifestyles of the disciples. These men did not start out in life as a group of what we would consider to be "saints." These were rough men; tax collectors, fishermen, etc. They were not well liked, and most of them were not well educated. Take for an example the Apostle Peter. Peter was not considered to be very bright by the other disciples; in fact his friends (the other disciples) would refer to him as "rock head" because they considered him to be as dumb as a stone. It was painful to Peter to be made fun of by the other disciples. Yet, Jesus made Peter the head of His Holy Church.

Why would Jesus make the disciple who was considered by his peers to be the dumbest among them to be the head of the Christian church? The answer is quite simple. Most people miss the message and principles taught by Jesus because they get too analytical about spiritual matters. Peter did not do this. He was one of the few to this day who did not over intellectualize the teachings of our Lord.

The problem with Christianity today is that people try to be too intellectual about the teachings of our Lord, Jesus Christ. We try to be so darn clever and so strict that we take all of the love out of our Lord's message. In fact, if you listen to the way most preachers (including priests of my own church) teach the message given to us from God, none of us will make it to heaven. We have added so many requirements to the teaching that we have forgotten the two great commandments given to us by Christ, Himself. This is the result of us trying to be smarter than the "other guy" instead of listening with the heart.

Peter was not like this. He understood that the only way to see God was through the eyes of love. It was because of the simplicity of Peter that Jesus said, "Upon this rock I shall build my Church."

Byron became a winner because he learned how to love and how to forgive. He discovered that it is just not that important to be "right" all the time. He would rather spend his time being happy and feeling God's love all around him.

You can be a winner too. The way to become a winner is by acknowledging your own powerlessness and accepting into your daily life the unlimited power of God, making use of His Divine Guidance in all of your affairs. Ask God to do for you what you cannot do for yourself. Then go about your day looking to see what you can do for others.

Turn your will and your life over to the care of God and seek His will for you throughout the day. When you come across a situation that appears to be beyond your abilities, remember this saying, "I can't, God can, and I will let Him." Then relax, take a little retreat, if you will, and you will be surprised how the right answer will come to you seemingly out of nowhere. But we must know where the answer came from; it came from the giver of life Himself, God. Remember what Jesus said, "Not my will, but Thine be done" (Luke 22:42 KJV). When it comes to winners, you will not find a greater winner than Jesus.

Some people are of the belief that if you give up everything and follow God that you are in for a boring, "humdrum" life. They say, "If I do only God's will for me I will have to give up everything that is fun for me."

I can hardly begin to tell you how far from the truth this is. I am a priest. I have dedicated my entire life to doing God's will. Let me tell you, I have more fun in life than most people. That's right, I do not lead a boring life, not for a moment. My life is filled with love, humor, and joy. I have found that God has a wonderful sense of humor. His will for me is to experience life toy the highest degree. This does not mean that I do not ever experience pain in my life. In every life there are periods of pain. This is part of the human condition. I do not fear the pain and I do not let the pain dictate how I treat other people. I cannot change pain, so I give it to God. God does for me what I cannot do for myself. Then the pain becomes a blessing because I can use my experience as a tool to help others, and together we become a team of winners.

Being a winner does not mean you have found a way to get through life and never be faced with problems. And becoming a winner does not mean you will never make a mistake or a wrong decision. Being a winner means you take everything, the good and the bad, to God. It means you seek God's help and guidance in everything you do.

Jesus was a winner and He helped other people become winners too. In so doing He gave us a commandment, which we must follow if we are to be counted as a winner. This is what He told us to do, "Freely you have received, freely give" (Matthew 10:8 NIV).

If you are not willing to share freely of everything you have learned and have been given, then you have not learned how to be a winner. Instead you have become a walking encyclopedia of useless information. Knowledge is of no value unless it is applied. It is in giving this stuff away (including material possessions) for fun and for free that we wake up in conscious unity with the Father and discover that we are winners and that our every need has been met.

Now that you have been told a second time how to be-come a winner (we were told the first time by Jesus in the Holy Bible), what are you going to do with this information? Are you going to sit around and come up with rea-sons as to why this will not work for you? Or maybe you are sitting around playing games with your intellect, weighing the spiritual and/or metaphysical value and meaning, wondering if it makes any difference as to which church this information comes from. Or, will you get into action and begin practicing these principles in all of your affairs? Remember, you cannot think yourself into good living. You must live yourself into good thinking.

I encourage you to begin on your spiritual journey today. Don't put off becoming a winner until tomorrow. Don't wait for someone to give you their approval before you turn your will and your life over to the care of God. Be a winner today and share everything that you find along the way with the people that you meet. Join the fellowship of winners and know at last what it feels like to truly be a winner and to be free of the bondage of self. Surrender now and win a life of love, and you will never walk alone again. I look forward to meeting you on this great road of life.

Notes

Chapter Four

Let Go and Let God

"Praise the Lord, all you nations; extol him, all you peoples. For great is his love toward us, and the faithfulness of the Lord endures forever. Praise the Lord." (Psalms 117:1, 2 NIV).

All through the book of Psalms, the Psalter describes a God who is loving and just. He has a loving and exciting relationship with God, and he hides nothing from God. The Psalter does not give us a shame-based theology. Rather, he encourages us through his own example and experience that we are to take every part of our life before God.

The difference between the Psalter and most people is the fact he knows that there is nothing in his life that he can do without God's help. He has surrendered himself to this fact. I like the term, "Being strong enough to be weak." Until I was in touch with my own powerlessness I could not accept God's power working in my life. "For man this is impossible, but for God nothing is impossible." (Matthew 19:26 KJV). This means if I want my life to change for the better, I have to be in touch with a power that can solve all my problems. This means I need God!

But, why would God want to help me? Doesn't he have more important things to concern himself with than little ole me? After all, he has a universe to run.

Let me share with you what Jesus has to say on the subject. "Two sparrows are sold for a penny, and yet not one of them fall to the ground without your Father's will. And how much more important are you than these birds? But so far as you are concerned, even the hairs on your head are numbered. Therefore fear not; you are much more important than many sparrows!" (Matthew 10:29-31 Lamsa Translation).

God is always waiting to help us. But He helps us in His ways, not ours. God always has a solution that leads to the highest good for everyone involved. But oftentimes we want to run the show. We want to fix our problems ourselves and stick to our own designs and ideas on how things are to be done. When everything falls apart we become angry with God and make statements like, "If God is so loving, why doesn't He do something to help me?" or, "Maybe there really isn't a God. If He were here and cared anything about me, He would have fixed this problem by now!"

God is willing and able to help you. But, there are a few things you must do. First you must let go and let God do His stuff. I have a favorite poem that talks about this, it's called, "Broken Dreams," and it goes like this:

"As children bring their broken toys, with tears for us to mend, I brought my broken dreams to God, because He was my friend. But then, instead of leaving Him in peace so He could work alone, I hung around and tried to help, with ways that were my own. At last, I snatched them back and cried, 'How can you be so slow?' 'My child,' He said, 'what could I do? You never did let go.'" Author unknown.

The second thing we must do is believe that God has the right answer. We must be willing to have faith in the truth that God knows what will lead us to the highest good, and that He knows what is best for us, always.

Third, we must be patient. We must be willing to believe in God's perfect timing. You would not plant tomatoes in your garden and a week later dig them up and throw away the seeds because they were not growing fast enough, would you? So it is when you plant a seed of faith.

Let's examine this at length. The seeds you are planting are the prayers you say. The soil is your consciousness. Faith is what you water the seeds with. Perfect Divine Law is what acts upon the seeds as life, and manifestation is the end result. The life, which is inside the seed, is God desiring to be expressed. However, God operates in perfect form with Divine Law, which He created.

We are told in the book of Ecclesiastes, "To every-thing there is a season." (Ecclesiastes 3:1 Lamsa Translation). So, there is a time to pray, and a time to affirm. There is a time to take action, and a time to be still. And, there is a time to let go and let God, and simply be patient, knowing that "It is the Father's good pleasure to give you the kingdom" (Matthew).

Letting go and letting God is not a form of laziness. It is what I call, "Active releasing." When you give a problem to God to resolve, you become ready and willing to do the next indicated step. But you leave the results in God's capable hands. You get out of the way by discontinuing the mental gymnastics going on in your head. You get into a positive knowingness that God is now in charge of the situation, and you are waiting to serve God as He so directs you.

As I go about my Father's business, I take no thought as to where my supplies will come from, that is not my business. I do whatever it is that God places before me to do. Then I let go, and let God provide the means for my needs to be met. This is not some form of wishful thinking. Wishful thinking will not get the job done. It is a deep knowing that my Heavenly Father cares for me.

It is a trusting in Him who made the universe and is at the same time, the universe itself.

I let go because I know that God is far more capable of providing for my needs than I am. Thus, I simply, "Suit up, and show up." And leave the rest to God.

Notes

Chapter Five

Finding a God of Your Own Understanding

Many people are turned off by "religion" because they were told that it was not okay for them to ask questions about God, as well as, many other topics regarding "dogma." I can remember being a child with many questions about many different religions and religious issues. I was always getting into trouble for asking, "Why do we believe that?" These kinds of questions usually receive the response of, "We just do. Don't ask why." This was not simply the position of one church. I received this kind of response from many different churches of diverse denominations. I felt that I was being told that I was bad for asking questions about certain teachings instead of simply "accepting things on faith."

In looking back, as well as sharing my curiosities with fellow students and friends, I realize that some of our "Religious Leaders" did not have any more of a clue than I did. And they, too, had been told, "Don't ask questions."

I did not have much understanding of the position these poor souls were in, until I was ordained a priest and found that I was not given all of the answers in school.

I have come to the conclusion that if the chain is going to be broken, I had better get into the solution. This meant that I had to admit that there was more to spiritual growth than reading the Bible, studying commentaries and going to Mass. They say in the East, "When the Master points at the Moon, all the idiot sees is the finger." If I was truly going to learn about my relationship with and to God, I was going to have to turn within to where God truly is. Jesus said, "the kingdom of God is within you" (Luke 17:21). In other words, I discovered that it is an "inside job."

Each of us must take this journey into the depths of our souls in order to discover the truth about God. My friend Chuck Chamberlain used to say to me, "Life is learning to uncover, discover and discard." This I have found to be a pearl of wisdom.

It is important to understand that you cannot find your relationship with God by way of another person's formula. While you can certainly borrow from other's methods, in the end, you must find your own path, dance your own dance.

No one can tell you what God is in His entirety. In the East they say, "He who knows does not say. He who says does not know." Saint Thomas Aquinas said, "We cannot tell you what God is. We can only tell you what God is not."

The Sacraments of the Church are truly spiritual Rites, but each person must achieve their own inner experience with the Sacraments. Don't mistake dogma for the Sacrament. Dare to have your own, deep and enriching embodiment of the Eucharist. Take it into your very soul. Let it speak to you in your heart. Don't accept another's definition of what it is to mean for you. You can never have a personal experience with Christ when holding to someone else's beliefs. Especially if you truly do not hold that same belief in your heart.

I say to you, don't follow the crowd! Have the courage to allow God to reveal Himself in your life as He really is, not as a group of people would tell you to believe. Saint Paul went against every body he grew up with when he followed Jesus. He followed the God of his own understanding. Just as God revealed Himself to Paul, so will He reveal Himself to you when you stop trying to tell God who and what He is supposed to be according to the masses.

What I am trying to say is, the Sacraments work, but the dogmas don't. Why? Because God is very personal and cannot be defined by any person, book, religious sect or school of theology. God is bigger than all of these things. And gratefully bean say He is a lot kinder than we are!

When you have that one-on-one experience with the Divine, you will no longer need someone else to tell you about God. I was celebrating a Mass with my Bishop when I had this experience. Let me share it with you. My Bishop and I were in his personal chapel with maybe ten other people in attendance. We had celebrated the first parts of the Liturgy and the Bishop was giving the Homily. As I was listening to the Bishop I was also looking at a beautiful painting of Jesus holding a baby. All at once I was overtaken by God's love for me as His child. I was painfully aware of the fact that He called me to the Holy Priesthood not out of any virtue I possessed, but rather, despite my iniquities. He called me and said He could use me to do good in His name.

I was so moved that I could not speak. I wasn't even able to continue to assist with the Mass. All I could do was sit in my pew and weep. I was not sad. God had touched my soul. I had nothing left to say. His love said it all.

After Mass, my Bishop left me to be alone in the chapel for about an hour and a half. When he did return I tried to explain to him what had happened, but of course I could not, and still cannot, put into words just what happened in my soul. My Bishop then looked deep into my eyes and he said to me, "Ah, you have had the Christ experience. You have now gone from simply being ordained, to being a Priest." We cried together as he embraced me, for he himself had had the Christ experience and knew the things I had experienced which cannot, and will not be put into words. It is beyond all words and thoughts.

Each person must come to this experience in their own way, on their own path. You cannot get there using my formula. You must find your own. That very formula is in you right now, but you must dig deep to find it. You must be willing to throw up your hands and say, "I do not know what God is. God, reveal Yourself to me in my life in a way I will understand." He won't abandon you. He will bring you to new and deeper levels of knowingness. And you will not be able to describe to anyone what has happened to you, for words will always fail in the effort to encompass the Divine. But you will know truer than you have ever known before that you are alive, and it is good!

Notes

Chapter Six

An Inside Job

It would appear that as a "religious community" we have been taught to always look outside of ourselves in order to find God. This would include the reading of books, attending religious services, going to Bible studies, etc.

Let me state that there is nothing wrong with the participation in any of the above-mentioned activities. However, there comes a time when each of us must turn within if we are truly ever going to find God.

The purpose of prayer and meditation is to commune with God. Prayer should be not simply a petition to God for a favor, but rather an expression of gratitude for what He is already doing for us.

I believe that when we pray for God to do something for us with the attitude that we must beg and plead in order to persuade God to fulfill our need, we have just limited God's ability to take care of our every need. Jesus said, "Pray believing that you have received, and you shall have" (Matthew 21:22 My Translation). I believe what Jesus is telling us is that God is always willing to do for us. So we do not need to convince God that He should do something for us, because He is already willing. However, God can only do for us, through us. This means that it is not God we need to convince, but rather it is ourselves we need to persuade.

This means we need to take a look at our belief systems. This is part of the process of turning within. It is important that we understand that God can only give us that which we are willing to receive. So it is not God's mind that we need to change, but our own. I would like to direct your attention to the book of Matthew. We are told in the Gospel here, "Who among you if your son asked you for bread would give him a snake? Or if he asked you for drink would give him a stone? If you who are evil (in error) know how to give good gifts, how much greater would your Father in heaven give those who ask Him?" (Matthew 7:9-11). "Two sparrows are sold for a penny, yet not one of them falls that the Father knows not of, yet how much more precious are you than these birds. As far as you are concerned the hairs on your head are numbered" (Matthew 10:28-30).

To me, this does not sound like a God who would withhold anything from His children. We are all God's children! Somehow we have taken on the idea that we are His stepchildren. Thus, He will do more for His "real kids" than He will be inclined to do for one of us. Let me state this clearly, God does not have stepchildren. We are all, every one of us, His children.

So once again I must believe that the problem is not with God or His willingness to do things for His children. The problem resides in our beliefs about God and our level of acceptance of His gifts for us as His children.

If we are going to experience change on our spiritual path, then we are going to have to rethink everything we have been taught about God and our relationship to Him as His creation and beloved children. We are going to have to unlearn years of bad information regarding our relationship to our Creator. We are going to have to become open to a new experience with God, which goes beyond books and religions.

In Buddhist teaching it is thought that the two things that keep us out of the Garden of Paradise are fear and desire. Jesus gives us the same message in the story of the rich man who wants to know how to get into Heaven. Jesus tells him that he must give up all of those possessions that are so important to him, giving it all to the poor (caring for God's children) and follow Jesus (trust that God will provide for his needs as well). Here he must give up his fear and learn to depend upon God for all of his supply. And he must give up desire, for to desire something one must first not be in possession of it. Jesus tells us that everything that belongs to the Father is ours to make use of. Thus, desire is a belief that there can be something outside the realm of God that we must have in order to know happiness. The very thought is erroneous.

Henceforth, we must reexamine our core beliefs about God, His universe and His willingness to care for us as His beloved children. We must realize our relationship to the universe and learn our place as members of the family of God. We are all sons and daughters of the Most High. It is our job to act accordingly!

I am reminded of an Eastern story of the egg of the Golden Eagle, which was found by a farmer. Apparently the mother eagle fell upon misfortune and was unable to return to the nest to care for the egg. So the farmer took the egg into the henhouse and placed it under a chicken in the hopes that the egg would eventually hatch.

After a few weeks of the hen sitting on the egg, it did indeed hatch along with the eggs of the other chicks. Even though the eagle looked different, the hen raised the eagle as one of her own. So the eagle learned to scratch at the ground for food and never learned to fly, for the mother being a chicken was not a bird of flight.

One day while the eagle was in the farmyard scratching for food with his adopted brothers and sisters, a great golden eagle flew over the farm. With amazement he watched as the eagle gracefully stretched out its wings and glided with the wind. With great reverence and awe he asked, "What kind of bird is that?" The chickens around him said, "That is an eagle, and he belongs to the sky. We are chickens and we belong to the ground, for we have not been given the gift of flight." And so the little golden eagle went back to scratching the ground for food like the other chicks did, for while in his soul he was an eagle, in his mind he was just a farmyard chicken.

Don't accept another's limitations as your own. Let your heart take flight. Let your soul move you to new heights, or are you just another farmyard chicken?

Notes

Chapter Seven

What Is Hell? What Is Heaven?

Quite often I am asked by people, "If God is all loving, why does He put people in hell?" This is a very good question. In order to answer this question it will be necessary for me to explain what Jesus meant when He talked about hell.

First of all let me say that "hell" is not a geographical place. This might sound strange to some people. What Jesus was talking about is a state of being that is the result of our actions and our fears. I call hell the sense of conscious separation from God. This does not mean that we are ever truly separated from God, for in reality we can never be separated from that which created us. I have heard it expressed like this, "God is in everything. And everything is in God." This is the truth of our being in reality. However, in our mind, our consciousness, we can feel as though we have been separated. This is a feeling, not reality.

Jesus made reference to a place outside of the city, which was also called "Hell" by the people. This was the place where the people of the city took their trash to burn for the purpose of sanitation. Thus, what we call "burning in hell" is really a sanitation process of our spiritual path. We do not go someplace for this burning. What this expression means is that we are burning within ourselves because we know that our actions are not of the highest good.

I want to be clear about this point. When we do something that is considered "wrong" God does not hold anything against us. It is we who hold these mistakes against ourselves. We are the last to forgive us. And we cannot get out of hell until we do forgive ourselves.

I would like to relate a personal experience with you. An example of how I held myself in hell for many years without knowing that I was my own captive. Some years ago I held a job in Los Angeles. At that time I resided in Fontana, California. That gave me a seventy-three mile drive to work each day. This was a long trip, which gave me a lot of time to live inside my head, so to speak.

One day I was driving to work and thinking about my life and of the days when I was growing up. I thought about things I had said as a child, which I thought were stupid. I thought of things I had done that I had regretted; relationships that had gone wrong, etc. With each thought I said to myself, "Man that was stupid, what an idiot. No wonder you haven't gone further in life. No wonder all of your relationships fail." Finally I yelled out at the top of my voice, "For God's sake, I was just a kid, I didn't know any better!" At that moment I knew who was keeping me in hell. It was not God. It was I. You see God had never stopped loving me. I stopped loving myself. God did not put me in hell for my sins. I did. God has always forgiven me. I needed to learn how to forgive myself.

I do not know of any "Hell" hotter than when one looks in the mirror and despises their own reflection. You may be saying to yourself right now, "This does not apply to me." It is my hope that it doesn't. However, most people walking around on this planet condemn themselves at one time or another for not being "good enough."

There are many people who have been raised with a shame-based theology who live in their own private hell on a daily basis, hoping that some day when they die they will leave this "vale of tears" and go to "Heaven." They have not been taught that Heaven and Hell are right where we are. You do not have to die to get to either place.

Again, it is important to have an understanding of the culture and the idioms of the language, which Jesus spoke when He was speaking of Heaven and Hell. These are levels of consciousness He was talking about.

Jesus also talked about Heaven. If there is not a place called "Hell," what about Heaven? Heaven is no more of a geographical place than Hell. Jesus was describing what I like to refer to as conscious unity with God. The next question is of course, how do I achieve this conscious unity with God? Is that even possible without dying? I have found that dying is not the only path to conscious unity. This is why Jesus said, "The Kingdom of God is at hand." The path to "Heaven" is an inside job. As we turn within to find the "Kingdom of God," we discover that what we have been looking for all of our life, we have been looking with. It is like trying to find your glasses - when you are wearing them.

I would like to share with you a story that my friend Chuck Chamberlain used to tell me when I was young. I do not know where Chuck got this story, but I think it says a lot. There were three fish swimming in the bay of Laguna. They were not doing too much, they had already eaten breakfast, they were just milling around when this great fish swam up to them and said, "Good morning, boys, isn't the water grand this morning?" And he swam off. One fish looked at the other and said, "The old boy talked about water. Have you ever heard of this water?" "No," the other fish replied. So, the first fish asked the third fish, "Have you heard about this water?" He said, "I know it must exist, because the great fish said there was water. Maybe we should look for this water." So they swam the seven seas in search of the water in which they lived, moved and had their being.

So it is with us. We go through our entire life in search of God, in which we live, move and have our being. So again I say, what you are looking for, you are looking with.

Jesus never went outside of Himself to find God because He knew that He was looking through the eyes of God. He told us that we are to do the same thing. He said, "The Kingdom of God is within you." And so it is.

This is another little story relating to Heaven and Hell I would like to share with you. I don't remember where I picked this story up, but it carries with it some wonderful clues as to how we can create our own Heaven or Hell.

A man had a dream one night that he died and was greeted by Saint Peter. The Holy Saint told the man, "I am going to show you two rooms. One is 'Heaven,' and the other is 'Hell'. You decide which room you belong in." So as they approached the first room Peter said, "This is the room we call Hell." When they entered the room the first thing the man noticed was that there was a great table of delicious food with people seated all around the table. Each of the people who were seated at the table had long forks, but their elbows could not bend, thus, they were starving, and there was great hunger and the gnashing of teeth, for they longed to eat of the wonderful food. Peter said again, "This is Hell."

Saint Peter then took the man to the next room and said, "This is Heaven." When the man entered the room he saw the same table with the same delicious food.

Again, the people had the long forks and elbows that could not bend. But, these people were feeding one another and having a party.

One cannot experience the joy of Heaven without also seeking to improve the quality of life for the people in this world who are all around them. Spend your life doing for others without the concern of "What's in it for me?" And you will not have to ask directions on how to get to Heaven. You will simply discover that you have been there all the time. And now you know it.

I would encourage you to stop looking to some place far away and outside of your own soul to find Heaven and Hell. Within your own consciousness you hold the keys to the "Kingdom." But you also hold the keys to "Hell." It is up to you to decide which door you are going to choose to unlock with the keys of your soul. You have been invited to come and sit at the table here in Heaven. Will you be joining us?

Notes

Chapter Eight

Race Consciousness

I use the term "race consciousness" to mean the belief system of a community, a nation and the entire world population as a whole. Race consciousness affects all of the human population and is manifested as the condition that the world in general is in. This affects world peace, famine, politics, and global relations.

Gandhi once said in an interview, "Until each person is in touch with the part of themselves that is willing to have violence, we cannot have peace." Gandhi made a powerful statement about race consciousness when he said this. The whole world is suffering from fear. Each nation seems to view other nations as competition. We hold to the idea that we have to get them before they get us. This is a global sickness that must be healed. But how? I have heard it said that when one person raises their consciousness in the least bit, they raise the consciousness of the community around them as well. I like what Walt Disney said, "It's a small world after all."

As long as we have the attitude of "there is us and there is them" we cannot help but to continue to operate out of fear. There are three acronyms for the word fear, (1) false evidence appearing real. (2) Forget everything and run. (3) Face everything and recover. We must begin to "face everything and recover" if we are going to have world peace. This is the only way to stop hunger on a global level. It is we who must change these things.

Gandhi was right. We must all look within ourselves and find that part of our consciousness that is willing to let others go hungry, that part of us that says bigotry is acceptable. We should heed the words of a song that is sung in many churches, which says, "Let there be peace on earth and let it begin with me." Global changes begin on an individual basis. It takes courage to look within one's own consciousness and honestly search for the thoughts and beliefs that need to be changed. It is much easier to look at our neighbor and point out their faults. But this will not do if we want to change the world vision and work to heal race consciousness. Some of my friends say it like this, "Keep doing what you are doing. Keep getting what you are getting."

Some people ask, "If things are so bad, and God is all powerful and wise, why doesn't He fix it?" I am reminded of a little story that goes something like this: A man was talking to God one day, and during this conversation he said to God, "There is so much suffering in this world, children are hungry, many people are homeless, etc. Why don't you do something about it?" God was silent all that day, and all that night. The next morning when God spoke to the man, He said, "I did do something, I made you."

The Universe is based on perfect Law. Divine Law. One Of these laws is that God never interferes with "free will." God does not break His own laws. But, if you think about it with any depth, He doesn't need to break His own laws because they are perfect. You see He gave us the power to make all of the necessary changes to make everything work.

God is not varying. He is always consistent. When He gave us free will He honored His gift. With this free will He also gave us brains to use. It is now time for us to start using them.

We have the power to change the world and heal race consciousness. You already have the desire. If you did not share in this desire you would not be reading this book. But please do more than read this book and the many books that share the same message; get into action. Put to work the principles laid out in this book. Practice these things in all of your affairs. Let the changes begin with you and in you. Don't let your fear keep you from being a hero. You have the power right now to make a good start. The power of God is within you. Use it to the highest good. Stand up and be counted as one who has found enlightenment. When you light a candle in a dark room and then light a second candle, the second candle does not detract from the first and make less light. No, they work together to make the room a brighter place. Let your light shine. You are a light unto the world. Help others to discover their light and bring a new brightness unto the world. For this you were born.

Notes

Chapter Nine

The Greatest of These Is Love

I truly believe that Jesus' greatest attribute was his ability to love, His unyielding capacity to love his fellow despite their faults. This is the kind of love we shall need to manifest in our lives if we are ever truly going to find serenity.

There are many people going through life in search of love. Every morning they wake up feeling totally alone. Or even worse yet are those who are married to someone they are supposed to be in love with and are still totally alone. I cannot think of a more painful loneliness than the latter scenario.

I can remember talking to a close friend of mine one time after taking stock of my life. I told him that I had found what had been missing in my living experience. He asked me what it was. I said, love. All my life I never had the sense that somebody loved me. I had spent my entire life, up unto that point, feeling completely alone. He asked me, "Do you want love in your life?" I said yes, more than anything I wanted to have love in my life. He said, "Here is what I want you to do. From this point on, I do not want you to ever go out looking for love. Love is not something that you get. It is something that you give. When you go out looking for love you come back empty. When you go out to give love you come back overflowing." He was right.

From that time to this I have not felt alone. Today I have love in my life.

Many of you reading this book know all too well what I am talking about. You have been on your own search each day, wondering if you will ever find "true love." I just gave you the secret to having love in your life. It works. It really works.

We must come to a point in our spiritual development where we learn to love everyone. Each person is born a child of God. This does not mean that we approve of their actions. But that we recognize that God is within them as much as He is in you and me. Jesus said, "Love those who despise you and persecute you." (Matthew 6:44) It is easy to love those who love you. Anybody can do that. I challenge you to bring yourself to love the homeless beggar on the street. The one that most look at with repose as they say under their breath, "Why don't you get a job, you bum?" What do you think Jesus would say to us with our greater-than-thou attitude? I think he has already given us his response. "What you do unto the least of these you do also unto me." It is our job to look into the eyes of our fellow man and see the face of God.

This chapter is not about bringing a feeling of guilt to people who have been unkind to those who are destitute. I do not think that God is about guilt. The point that I am trying to make is this. If you want more love in your life you must become more loving. My friend Chuck Chamberlain used to say to me, "You are what you are giving away. If you are giving away love, you are love today, if you are giving away hate, you are hate today." Most spiritual teachers have said it like this, "As it is within, so it is without."

Remember, all thought is creative. If you are holding hate in your consciousness, hate will be manifested in all of your affairs.

If it is love you are holding in your consciousness, love will be your reward. This is one of the principles of Divine Law. You cannot plant watermelon seeds and get radishes. What you sow is what you will harvest. Again, this is the secret to having love in your life.

A man once asked Jesus, "Which of the commandments is the greatest?" Jesus answered, "Love thy Lord your God with all your mind, with all your soul and with all of your might. And the second is like unto it, love your neighbor as yourself." If we did as Jesus commanded us to do, we would not have time to do anything but love God. Really what we have been practicing here on earth is prejudice. Case in point. If you say "I love you" to one person, yet you say about another person, "I don't love this other one," your love for the first person is not real, it is simply prejudice. Love does not know one person from another. It must love all people equally.

When we learn to love the people we do not like, we will have found true freedom. This is the kind of freedom that cannot be taken away from us by anyone or anything. God's whole plan for mankind is based on love. We have been created by God for the purpose of giving greater expression to love. And God does not love one group of people more than He does another. This is opposite of what a lot of religions teach. There are so many groups who claim that they have the only way to God's love and approval. Every other religious group is going to Hell. This is not what was taught by Jesus. The first response I usually get as a retort to my statement is this: "It is written in book of John, 'I am the way, and the truth and the life. No one comes unto the Father but by me.' " It sounds like they have me here, doesn't it? Let me offer some enlightenment here. This quote from Jesus is a typical Aramaic expression. In the idioms of the Aramaic language this statement would mean, no one can find their true relationship with God without using the principle I am teaching. Jesus was not trying to glorify His personality. He was giving us His secret to finding God. What was that secret? It is the same secret that has been taught by every spiritual Master. "Love thy Lord your God with all your heart, all your mind and with all your might. And love your neighbor as yourself." This was the message of Jesus. It was not all who believe in His personality are going to Heaven.

If God only loved Christians He would not be perfect love. Thus, He would cease to exist. God loves all of His creations. He is perfect! It is man who has misunderstood the teachings of the Master. Part of the problem stems from the lack of knowledge of the idioms of the Aramaic language by Western world theologians. I am not putting these people down, I am stating a fact.

God is the world's greatest lover. He is perfect in all of His ways. He is not petty, as we seem to be. We are to apply the qualities of God into our everyday lives. Instead, what we have done through the years is to project our prejudices unto God and then say, "Because I do not like these things or teachings or this group of people, God doesn't like them either." These are our prejudices, not God's. God knows only love, not hate. "Faith, hope and love. But the greatest of these is love." (1 Corinthians 13:13)

Notes

Chapter Ten

Affirmative Prayer

Jesus tells us that when we pray, we are to believe that we have already received the thing we are praying for and we will have it. The first question that comes to most people's minds after reading this statement made by Jesus is, "How am I supposed to believe I have received something when I cannot see the item in front of me. If I already had this thing I would not be praying for it in the first place. What kind of double talk is this?" It is not "Double talk." Jesus was explaining one of the laws of the Universe.

Let me take some time to explain the importance of this principle. This is the key to getting your needs met on a day-to-day basis. First of all, it is important that you understand that every serious thought is a prayer. It is a prayer either for something you want to happen, or for something you don't want to happen. Every thought is creative. Whatever you think about most is what you will experience in your life. If you are always saying that there is not enough money to go around, you will be right. Without knowing it you have just created the manifestation of poverty.

Conscious thought is more powerful than unconscious thought. This means that God has given you the power to change your experience. But this means you will need to be willing to change your entire life. A friend of mine says it like this, "Keep

doing what you are doing, and keep getting what you are getting."
My friend is right. However, until the pain gets great enough, most
of us are not that motivated to make the necessary changes in
the way we live. It is not enough to merely start off our day with a
few chosen affirmations. We must inventory our entire life, as well
as our belief systems. This is not an overnight process. But all it
takes is the willingness to change and some beginning footwork
for us to start getting some results.

One problem that a lot of people have in starting on this
new road of conscious awareness is that after they start to get
some results they go back to the way they did things before. And
then they wonder what happened. You cannot think yourself into
good living. You must live yourself into good thinking. It is not the
Universe or God that is in need of change. It is our attitude about
God and His spiritual Universe that must change. If you think you
are the child of an unfriendly God, living in an unfriendly Universe
that will be your experience. As it is in your consciousness, so it
is in your living experience. I cannot state this principle strongly
enough.

To have more, you must be more in the thoughts you hold
in your consciousness. It is not God, or an unfriendly Universe,
that is keeping your good from you. It is the thoughts that you are
holding about yourself, which is the dividing wall that is between
you and your desired good. You must get past some of the following ideas: "I do not deserve this good thing." "It is a sin to ask
God for nice things, therefore, I am bad for even wanting this thing
in the first place." "It is more noble to go without things." "If I have
nice things I am a glutton." Etc.

This is not what Jesus taught us about our loving Heavenly
Father who is perfect. No, this thinking will not do. Jesus told us
that, "It is the Father's good pleasure to give you the kingdom."

(Luke 12:32) "However, God can only do for us, through us. So it is our job to clear the path and become an empty vessel for God to fill us with His good.

One of the reasons people tend to not receive the thing they are praying for, whether it be a prayer for a healing of health, a healing in a relationship, a healing in finances, or any other kind of need, is because they follow up their prayer with fear. Remember, all thought is creative. Each time you pray and then spend time worrying about the result, you have just canceled out your prayer with your fear. Fear is a type of faith. In fact most people have more faith in failure than they do in success. Thus, fear is the stronger thought. My friend Jack White used to quite often say to me, "If you're going to pray, why worry? And if you're going to worry, why pray?" He was so right. To get the results we are looking for we must begin to trust that the Universe and God are on our side.

Every time Jesus prayed He never doubted for a moment that His prayers would be answered. He knew that God was always willing to fulfill the requests made by Jesus. When Jesus went to the tomb of His friend Lazarus He said, "I know you always hear my prayers." Then He said, "Lazarus, arise." And Lazarus came forth out of the tomb.

The first thing people say to me when I give this quote is, "That was Jesus, and He is the Lord. I am just an ordinary person." I would like to direct your attention to another thing that Jesus said. "These things I have done, ye shall do also" (John 14:12). He also told us that the Father with Him, is also within us. So if we believe as Jesus believed, and pray as He prayed, we will get the results that Jesus did. Jesus did not even need to be present for the manifestation to take place. Case in point. A Centurion came to Jesus because his son was gravely ill. When He approached

Jesus he said, "Just say the word and my son will be healed." I want for you to pay attention what Jesus said to him. "By your faith he has been healed." When the Centurion returned home his son was healed. Two very important points that should be made are: (1) Jesus did not need to go to the home where the boy lay ill. (2) Jesus told the man that "By his faith his son was healed."

The Centurion had no question in his mind that if Jesus spoke His word his son would be healed. This is the kind of faith we need to have with regard to the word we speak whenever we pray. When we place that much faith into our spoken word, we will see the manifestation of that spoken word. This is the Law of the Universe. It is unwavering in its application. It works the same way every day. It is unchangeable. It does not work one way one time and another way the next time it is used. It is a perfect Law. That is why it is so important to heed the wise saying, "As a man thinketh in his heart, so is he."

In the book of Genesis we are told that we were made in the "Image and likeness of God." This means that just like God we have the ability to co-create. We are called "Children of God." And to add to this point, Jesus said, "Have I not told you ye are gods?"

The point I am trying to make here is a simple one. When praying, we should speak our word with authority; after all, we are children of the Most High. It is our job to start acting like God's children. This means we are to be in partnership with God. Of course He is the senior member of this partnership. I have a friend who named his business "H.P. and Son," meaning Higher Power (God) and son. Needless to say it is a successful business. He has learned to do all things to the glory of God.

We need to get away from the idea that we are down here doing the best we can while God is "Up in heaven somewhere" sitting on His throne, taking notes of all of our mistakes; and is unwilling to help us get through this "vale of tears." We are not victims of God. We are children of God. This means we have been given power. But we must remember that this power comes from God the Father and that He is the power that He has given us.

Everything we need in order to be happy, God has already placed here. In fact the gift from God was made in the foundation of the earth. This means that the power necessary to make life enjoyable has been granted us. It is called our conscious thought. I like something Richard Bach said in his book titled Illusions. He says, "You are never given a dream without also being given the means to make it come true." All true dreams and desires come from God. When we are praying and asking God to make our dreams come true, giving Him a list of reasons why it would be a good idea to do this "thing" for us and telling Him this idea, if made manifest, will help so many people, we are working from the idea that God is not willing for us to have our dreams and goals fulfilled. Again I would like to state, it is not God's mind that needs to be changed, but our mind. God is always willing to give us the things we need in order for us to live up to our highest potential. Speak your word with authority, knowing that it is God's good pleasure to give you the kingdom. Remember who you are when you are praying. You are the child of the Most High. God does not have stepchildren. What He is willing to do for one of His children, He is willing to do for all of His children. This means He is just as willing to do these things for you as He did for Jesus the Christ.

When praying, always look for the highest good in every situation. Pray always in the spirit of love. Look beyond the simple good that you shall receive and see how you can benefit the world around you with your dreams and goals. In so doing, you will find the greatest level of joy in everything you undertake. And remember, God is always for you, supporting you all the way. It is His will that you should be happy and have the things that bring you joy and the greater expression of love. This is part of learning how to pray affirmative prayers and receiving into your life the manifestations that lead to a greater experience in living.

Notes

Chapter Eleven

Resentment, a Cancer to the Soul

Jesus gives to us what seems to be a tall order. He tells us to love those who despise us, do good to those who have done evil deeds against us, and if someone slaps you on the right cheek, turn to him your left. This is not normally the first response most people have when being offended by another person. In fact, most people like to live life by the rule of the Old Testament, "An eye for an eye, and a tooth for a tooth." Why would Jesus ask us to do something that seems to go totally against how we feel inside?

Jesus understood that resentments are the cancer that eats away at the soul. Resentments keep us from feeling the presence of God in our everyday life. If we are going to know God, we must be free of our resentments.

Most resentments are seeded in fear. Fear of what? Fear of, "Not looking good," fear of losing something that is important to us (job, relationship, money, social status, self-esteem, etc.), fear we may not get something we want. These are just a few fears.

A majority of the problems in this world today are the result of fear transformed into resentment. We have learned to base our level of happiness on the performance and actions of other people.

When these people do not perform according to our expectation, we become angry and discontent. The more we think about how that person or group of people have let us down (whether real or fantasized), the angrier we become. Now we have resentment.

Resentments are like a slow-moving poison. A resentment held in one's own consciousness kills the body through forms of disease such as high blood pressure, heart attacks, ulcers, various forms of cancer, ad infinitum.

In addition to acting as a poison to the body, resentment takes the life and love out of marriages, friendships, and business relationships, just to name a few important relationships. But, even more than these, resentments rob us of our true relationship with God. When you are filled with resentments, you cannot feel that sense of being one with God in love. If for no other reason than this, we must gain freedom from resentments in order to have conscious contact with God.

I have watched entire families torn apart by unresolved resentments. Some of these resentments were the result of miscommunication where one person misunderstood something another person said, and instead of asking for clarification, they chose to take the path of self-righteous anger, and assumed they knew what the other meant by their statement. I have witnessed friendships of many years destroyed in this fashion.

I had a friend who allowed a resentment to ruin his relationship with his daughter. This story is a prime example of what we have been talking about. When his daughter was twelve years old, my friend, whom we shall call Harold, was in a hospital being treated for alcoholism. During a conversation with his daughter at the hospital, Harold thought his daughter said he was stupid. From that day until his death (some twenty years later) he only spoke to his daughter one time.

I realize that this is an extreme example. However, I could write an entire book just on cases I have heard while doing Pastoral Counseling with families that have been ripped apart as the result of unresolved resentments. A dead relationship is a pretty high price to pay in order to be "right" all of the time. But our ego says, "Go ahead, pay the price. We were looking for a relationship when we found this one." "Boy, are they going to be sad after I am gone."

Resentment is one of Satan's greatest tools. Nothing brings about a greater sense of conscious separation from God than a well-justified resentment. From this all forms of spiritual disease stem.

If you want to experience a life that is filled with love, peace and joy, you must be free of resentments, even those resentments that appear to be totally justified and warranted. This means you are going to have to take some action in order to find this freedom I am talking about.

We cannot dissolve a resentment by simply, "Affirming peace." Footwork must be taken in order to find true inner peace. Let us start by getting out of the mind frame of "Who's right?" and start getting into the openness of the idea of "What is right." Examine the situation by writing about your resentment. Ask yourself, "What am I really angry or hurt about?" "What is it that I fear in this situation?" "What is my part in all of this?" "What can I do to resolve this situation that will bring healing for everyone involved?"

Now comes the hard part. Pray for the reason or persons whom you resent. Pray for their welfare, that their lives be filled with love, peace, joy and prosperity. Pray these prayers for a few weeks and you will find yourself coming to mean the well wishes you are praying for. Ask for guidance and direction in where you can bring peace and forgiveness into the situation. Ask God to remove the bitterness from your heart, that you may at last be free of the bondage of hate.

I remember Dr. Victor Frankl saying in a lecture that he came across a man he had been a prisoner with in the concentration camps in Germany during the reign of Hitler. He asked the man if he ever thought about their days in the camp during the war? The man answered and said, "I think of it every day, and I damn those Nazis to hell!" Dr. Frankl said, "Then you are still their prisoner."

If you are tired of being a prisoner of another or to a situation, try using the exercise I outlined in this chapter. Most people who have made use of this practice have found for themselves a personal freedom that is priceless. They discover they are no longer a hostage of their own anger and resentments. They find that this world and its people no longer dominate their lives. And the greatest discovery of all is the closeness they feel in their relationship with God. They have found the key that unlocks the door to that place in their heart that I call "Conscious unity with God."

Notes

Chapter Twelve

The Beatitudes Long Form

In the famous Sermon on the Mount given by Jesus we are given the keys to success in one of Jesus' most quoted lessons. I would like to examine each one of these "lessons" one by one and give you a new perspective on these sayings as the result of shedding new light on them with the use of the idioms of the language spoken by Jesus. The section of the Bible we will be discussing comes from the book of Matthew, chapter 5, and verses 3 through 9.

Blessed are the poor in spirit: for theirs is the kingdom of heaven. It would be a closer translation to say, Blessed are the poor in pride: for theirs is the kingdom of heaven. What Jesus is telling us is that you need to be humble in order to enter into the kingdom of heaven and know peace. I like the expression, "Do you want to be right? Or do you want to be happy?" The humble yield their will to God, knowing that God wants them to live up to their highest potential. It is only in a state of complete humility that we can find a sense of conscious unity with God.

Blessed are they that mourn: for they shall be comforted. Let us consider whom Jesus was speaking to when He gave this deep and compassionate lesson. He was speaking to a group of people who were oppressed. They had lost their land, as well as loved ones who were sold into slavery. They were lamenting. Jesus is saying, "God knows your pain, and He has sent to you a comforter." The comforter is the bearer of the Holy Truth about our kinship to God. He will teach you to have no fear for what man can do unto you. But know that God who is perfect shall bring you comfort and peace through the truth of a spiritual universe.

Blessed are the meek: for they shall inherit the earth. Jesus used the word meek, not the word weak. The true meaning of the word meek is humble. Jesus was explaining to these people the importance of humility. A humble person does not take credit for the good things in their life. They know that all good gifts come from God. Thus, they give credit where credit is due. This is an important lesson Jesus gave to the world. If we would only pay close attention to what He told us, we would experience more good gifts in our everyday living experience. The message here is, "Stop trying to run the entire show." If you want to have more good in your life, do the footwork, but leave the results up to God. Jesus said, "Not my will, but Thine be done." I have a little prayer that I say when I am going into a crisis situation such as an Emergency Room or a major disaster. This is my simple prayer: "God, I'll peddle, you steer." This prayer says it all for me. It says I am willing to do the footwork and follow the directions given to me by God. I am not running the show. I am simply suiting up and showing up. All of the "good works" are the result of God's wisdom. This is what Jesus was telling us. Be humble and you shall be open to receive all that the Father has to give to you for you understand that He is the source of your good, and that all things are done by His power working through you.

Blessed are they which do hunger and thirst after righteousness: for they shall be filled. I like the expression, "Blessed are they which hunger and thirst after Right-consciousness." All who truly seek to know their right relationship with God shall receive the enlightenment they are seeking. However, there is a condition put upon this search. The seeker must be seeking with the motivation of truly wanting to know God's will for them, and not be in search of fulfillment of the ego. If you are seeking spiritual principles and righteousness out of the motive of trying to get more "things" in your life or so you can feel more powerful, you are fooling yourself, but you are not fooling God. You can never fool God. However, it is quite easy for someone to fool himself or herself. The true motive for hungering and thirsting after righteousness is that earnest desire to become a clearer expression of God. It is best if one seeks only to be able to better do God's will. This is what it means to truly hunger and thirst after righteousness. If this is what you are looking for, you shall be filled.

Blessed are the merciful: for they shall obtain mercy. You are what you are giving away. If you want mercy in your life, you must first be merciful toward other people. Jesus said in His famous prayer, "And forgive us our trespasses, as we forgive those who trespass against us" (Matthew 6:12). He gave us the secret to finding mercy. A friend of mine says it like this, 'You cannot keep it unless you give it away." This is the meaning of the saying of Jesus.

Blessed are the peacemakers: for they shall be called the children of God. This is a statement that I wish all religious leaders, as well as all world leaders could hear and understand. God is a God of peace, not a God of war. All too often nations and their peoples have gone off to war "in the name of God." How long will it take before we as a world will come to the realization that God does not love one set of His children more than He does another. We are all His kids. God does not have stepchildren! The peacemaker is the person or persons who understand this principle and treat everyone around him or her with love and respect. If we are truly followers of Jesus the Christ, we need to follow His instruction. He told us to, "Love your enemies, bless them that curse you, do good to them that hate you, and pray for them which despite-fully use you, and persecute you; that you may be the children of your Father which is in heaven: for He maketh His sun to rise on the evil and the good and sends rain on the just and the unjust. For if you love them which love you, what is your reward? Do not the publicans do the same? And if you salute your brethren only, what do you do more than others? Do not the publicans do so? Therefore, be perfect, even as your Father which is in heaven is perfect" (Matthew 6:44-48, my translation).

Jesus did not say, "Love only those who are Christians or may become Christians." He told us to love all people including those whom you would call your enemy. This is the real test of our spiri-tuality. It is easy to love and be kind to those who share the same religious views and beliefs that you hold to be true. However, what separate the "Sunday morning Christians" from the wholehearted followers of the Holy teachings of Christ Jesus is the willingness and ability to see God in everyone regardless of their religious af-filiation, and to serve all people out of the motive of love. This is what Jesus taught.

God would never pit one of His children against another. The very idea that God could be so evil is absolutely insane. Only a sick mind could think such a thing. It is this kind of person who needs our prayers for the healing of their mind and spirit.

It is now time to get out of "who is right," and time to get into "what is right." And what is right? The understanding that we are all God's children. That is what is right. "Blessed are the peace-makers: for they shall be called the children of God."

Notes

Chapter Thirteen

No Man Can Serve Two Masters

Jesus tells us in the sixth chapter of the book of Matthew, verse twenty-four, "No man can serve two masters: for either he will hate the one, and love the other; or else he will hold to the one, and despise the other. You cannot serve God and Mammon."

Jesus understood the law of perfect supply. He went about His Father's business and took no thought for what He needed to survive in life. He knew that God would see to His every need.

All too often do I see people wasting their life away chasing the old "Yankee dollar." Their whole life is centered on making money so that they can "keep up with Joneses." When you ask them about what they would like to get out of life they will usually answer, "I would like to live long enough to build up a good retirement and then spend the rest of my life doing the things I enjoy."

This is what happens when you spend your life serving mammon. Don't get me wrong. There is nothing wrong with having money. The question is, is your money serving you, or are you serving your money?

Jesus was a positive thinker. He believed in great possibilities. He could do this because He knew that God was the source of

His supply. Jesus spent His life serving God, and never did he go without the things that were necessary. He told us that God would take care of our needs just as He took care of the needs of Jesus. This is what Jesus said, "I tell you, do not worry about your life, what you will eat or drink; or about your body, what you will wear. Is not life more important than food, and the body more important than clothes? Look at the birds of the air; they do not sow or reap or store away in barns, and yet your Heavenly Father feeds them. Are you not much more valuable than they? Who of you by worrying can add a single hour to his life? And why do you worry about clothes? See how the lilies of the field grow. They do not labor or spin. Yet I tell you that not even Solomon in all his splendor was dressed like one of these. If that is how God clothes the grass of the field, which is here today and tomorrow is thrown into the fire, will He not much more clothe you, O you of little faith? So do not worry, saying, 'What shall we eat?' Or 'What shall we drink?' Or, 'What shall we wear?' For pagans run after all these things, and your Heavenly Father knows that you need them. But seek first His kingdom and His righteousness, and all these things will be given to you as well" (Matthew 6:25-33 NIV).

If you get into your God-given life work, a couple of things are going to happen: 1. You will reap enjoyment in living. 2. You will fulfill a need in this world. Don't get caught up in worrying about the financial end of your life work. Jesus told us that if we follow God, and truly seek His will for us, our needs would be taken care of by God.

Case in point. I have one job in life. That job is to take care of God's kids. That is all I do. It is God's job to take care of me. God does not need me to tell Him how to do His job. And He provides me with directions on how to do my job.

You may be saying to yourself right now, "It's easy for you to go around taking care of God's kids, you're a Priest, and that's what you are supposed to be doing. I on the other hand have to work for a living in order to provide for my family." Let me respond by saying this. As an Orthodox Priest, I too, am married and have a family to provide for. Again I say, I have only one job in life and it is to take care of God's kids. While I am doing my job, God is doing His, which is to take care of me. Our vocations may be different, but the end result, as well as our motivation of our work must be the same if we are truly going to find the joy in living.

I did not always have this attitude. There was a time before my ordination when I served money instead of serving God. I thought that if I earned enough money I would be happy. I worked as a pressman, printing newspapers and made good money doing it. However, I was very unhappy. In fact I hated every day I went to work and my weekends were just as miserable because I knew I had to return to that job within a day or two. Being a pressman was not my life's work. For some people it is and, not only do they enjoy it, they provide an important service to the world around them.

When the pain of depression became great enough, I had to put money aside and ask myself (and God) what kind of work I should be doing instead. What was I born to do? It was then that I made a conscious decision to follow the dream that was placed in my heart by God. This dream is my life's work.

Don't make the mistake many people make of assuming that when you find your life's work there will be no more hard times or struggles. This simply is not true. I have had to work hard to achieve my goals. It is a labor of love, but nonetheless, I have had to do a lot of footwork along the way. There have been times when I have had to put my faith to work in order not to simply quit and give up on my dreams.

We all must do some footwork if we are going to attain our goals and find true happiness and joy. We are to be in partnership with God. In other words, we have to do our part. We must suit up and show up and not yield to fear.

Case in point. If you think that God is going to do everything for you without your part, doing the footwork, I have a little exercise for you to do. Try locking yourself into a closet, pray for a hot dog, and see if God sticks it through the keyhole.

God is more than happy for you to enjoy a hot dog, but it is up to you to get out of your seat and go get it. God is our Creator, not our bellhop. Yet, He does for us what we cannot do for ourselves.

Throughout this book I have given you the secret as to how you can experience more good in your life. However, I do not want to give you the impression that we can simply take, take, and give nothing back. This idea would not do!

Jesus gave us the answer to the question of what it is we must do, of what our part is to be. He told us to, "Seek first the kingdom of God and all its Righteousness and all of these things will be added unto you" (Matthew 6:33).

You cannot serve two masters, for a house that is divided against itself will fold. Therefore, serve only God. How do you serve only God? By taking care of God's children without worrying about what's in it for you. Be good to people for free and for fun because you want to. When you do this you put into action a Divine Law, which will bring to you a hundredfold the good you are giving away. Give and then forget the gift. After all, do you really think that you can out-give God? Think about this for a moment. You have to go to God for supplies you need. God doesn't need to go anywhere or to anyone to fulfill your need of supply, for He is the supply itself. He is the very source we seek. God is complete and whole within Himself. You cannot out give the gift Himself.

I quite often hear people say that they desire to have more good in their life. They are under the assumption that having more "things" will make them happy. I watch them buy a new car, and for a while the empty space in their gut feels full. But after a little time passes they are in search of something else to make them feel happy. So they buy a boat, then a jet ski, then a motor home, etc. What they fail to understand is that what they are really wanting is to experience more of God in their life.

Again, there is nothing wrong with having nice things in your life. The trouble begins for us when we start looking to "play toys" to make us happy. God is the source of all joy. If you seek to have conscious contact with God, you will find oneness with your source of joy, as well as have the things that bring fun into your living experience. Seek first the kingdom of God and all these things will be added to you.

Serving God does not mean living out your life in a "humdrum," boring and dull fashion. This is not God's will for us. God's will for us is that we should experience life in the highest degree. Jesus came that we should have life, and have it abundantly. In other words, God wants for us to have great joy in our everyday living experience.

I have had people tell me that I do not fit their preconceived idea of what a priest should be like. They tell me that I have too much fun in life. I tell jokes (I guess some people think that priests don't have a sense of humor) and laugh and spend my life playing with the rest of my Heavenly Father's children. We are told in Psalms 118:24, "This is the day the Lord has made; let us rejoice and be glad in it."

To serve God is to know joy. This is why I have so much fun in life. I have learned to not take myself too seriously. God has a wonderful sense of humor. How do I know this? It is very simple. If God did not have a sense of humor, I could not have a sense of humor, for humor is a gift from God to His children. Perhaps it is one of the finest qualities granted us from God. This is why I say, "Serve God. It is a great way to live." And for heaven's sake have fun. It makes God happy.

Notes

Chapter Fourteen

Living in Today

We are told in the book of Proverbs, "Do not boast about tomorrow, for you do not know what a day may bring forth" (Proverbs 27:1).

Too many times I see people get so caught up in the future that they lose out on everything that this day has to offer. They do not understand the importance of living life one day at a time.

I am not suggesting that you should not make plans for the future, if you saw my day planner you would notice that I have activities marked in as far in the future as a year from now. It's okay to plan for the future. But I take care of today's business today, and tomorrow's business tomorrow.

Another danger to our happiness that we face, which is just as hazardous as spending your whole day dreaming or worrying about the future, is getting stuck in the past.

I had an uncle whom I loved very much. In many areas of his life he was quite intelligent. However, he could not let go of the past. He would think of something that happened to him way back when he was eleven years old and he would become enraged all over again as though the incident just took place a few minutes ago. He would be angry for days at a time because of this.

I liken the reviewing of one's past to driving a car. In a car you have a rear view mirror. The purpose of the rear view mirror is to make it possible for you to glance at the things that are behind you. This is helpful for making changes from lane to lane and to assist in avoiding another vehicle hitting you from behind. When using the mirror, it is best to take short glances and then look forward. If you stay focused on the rear view mirror, eventually you are going to hit another car or some other object in front of you because you were so worried about the things behind you, which you are powerless over, that you cannot see the things that are ahead of you.

So it is with life. I believe that everyone should sit down at one time or another and review their entire life, looking for unhealthy patterns they have carried with them throughout their life to the present day. They should look to see where they may owe amends, and look to see where fear and selfishness have dominated their life. And then put the past where it belongs, behind them. You may from time to time glance into life's rear view mirror. Sometimes we can use some of the information from our past to help another person. But just take a glance. Don't get caught up and focused on reliving all the old past experiences.

If you are going to experience conscious unity with God, you have to get into today. "This is the day the Lord has made, let us rejoice and be glad in it" (Psalms 118:24). Your relationship with God is a here and now kind of thing. It is your job to suit up and show up. God is not far off in the future. He is here right now. "The kingdom of God is at hand [here now]" (Mark 1:15).

Today is the only day I have any power over. When I go to bed tonight I will review this day. I will ask myself if I lived out this day to the fullest, or was I stuck in tomorrow or yesterday? I will ask myself if I spent most of my time seeing what I could do for others or was I consumed with myself, a slave to my ego? I will try to keep my list current and focused on this day, for today was God's gift to me, and what I did with the day is my gift back to God.

This book would never get finished if I did not do today's writing today. Tomorrow I may not have the same things to say as I do today. I cannot say it enough. This is the day the Lord has made, make good use of it.

Today, choose to be happy. I once knew a man who used to always say, "When this thing happens, I will be happy. When I graduate from college, I will be happy. When I get that job I went to school for, I will be happy." And so on. One day this person woke up to what he was doing. He realized that he had been putting off his happiness. From that point on he made a decision every morning when he got out of bed to be happy "today." He would no longer postpone his joy. He learned the importance of staying in today.

Don't put off your relationship with God another day. Don't put off your joy till tomorrow. Don't hang on to your resentments of yesterday. Live, love, laugh and be happy today. And, if there are tears to be shed, then let them fall. But whatever you do, keep it in today.

I have found that there is no problem too large, no pain too great, and no challenge too powerful for me to handle with God's help one day at a time.

Notes

Chapter Fifteen

God, Love, and Marriage

In a time when the rate of divorce is so high, I think it is important that we discuss what makes for a healthy and successful marriage.

When people speak of marriage and what are the key ingredients that make for a lasting relationship, the first word that comes to most people's mind is love. What is this love stuff that must be present in a marriage? I say it is the expression of God. For what is God, but love?

I like what the Apostle Paul has to say regarding love. "Love is patient, love is kind. It does not envy, it does not boast, it is not proud. It is not rude, it is not self-seeking, it is not easily angered, it keeps no record of wrongs. Love does not delight in evil but rejoices with the truth. It always protects, always trusts, always hopes, always preserves. Love never fails" (1 Corinthians 13:4-8 NIV).

Somehow many people getting married today have been given the impression that a marriage license is a deed of ownership. I assure you it is not. Marriage is a commitment between two people that they are going to serve God through loving one another and doing things for one another for free and for fun.

I can remember talking one time to an old and dear friend. I had told him that I had discovered what the thing was that had been missing from my life. He asked, "What is it?" I said, "Love. I never knew what it was like to feel loved." He then asked me, "Do you want love in your life?" I told him, "Yes, more than anything. I can't stand to feel all alone anymore." He said, "Here is what I want for you to do. When we hang up the telephone I don't want for you to ever look for love again. Love is not something you get; it is something you give away. When you go out looking for love, you come back empty. When you go out giving love away, without a price tag, you come back overflowing with it."

My friend Eddie was right. From that time to this, I have never again been alone. There are many times that I am by myself, but never truly alone.

Do you want love in your marriage? Let me tell you a secret. Marriage is not a fifty-fifty deal. If you want your marriage to be filled with love and joy you must give one hundred percent of yourself and expect nothing in return. You cannot find joy in a relationship with a "I want, I don't want" attitude. Or, with the expectation that your spouse is there to take care of your every need. Nor will conditions on the other person to perform a certain way or the relationship will end approach, bring success to the relationship. Or here is my favorite expression I hear when meeting with couples whose marriage is headed for divorce court, "I am not doing anything for them until they do something for me." This way of thinking will sour the sweetest of relationships. It simply must be thrown out of your belief system, and out of your relationship.

One of the worst ideas, in my opinion, taught in a lot the so-called " self-help" books these days is this one, 'You have to love; yourself before you can love someone else." This is so backward to the way love really works that it is no wonder that so many people are going through divorces while they "learn to love themselves."

My friend Chuck Chamberlain, who was married to the same wonderful woman for well over fifty happy years, told me, "You are what you are giving away." If you want love in your relationships you must put it there. You must get out of yourself. It is by loving other people that we come to love our self. And why have we come to love ourselves? By loving other people for free and for fun, we ourselves have become loving and/or lovable.

A wise man once said, "To love another person is to see the face of God." Look for God in your spouse. Praise the good and let go of the bad. The Apostle Paul said, "Love keeps no record of wrongs" (1 Corinthians 13:5 NIV).

Love is a funny thing. You have to give it away in or-der to keep it. I have found that the more I do nice things for my wife without any expectations, the more I find that I am in love with her, and I find myself to be excited to be in the relationship.

I have also found it to be of great importance that the family learns to pray together. God is a good God, and should be expressed in every relationship. In speaking with hundreds of couples, I have found that in the majority of successful relationships the families prayed together, as well as worshiped together. In addition to family prayer, each member of the relationship practices his or her own spiritual principles. The practice of worship and prayer was not confined to one particular denomination. In fact, the couples I spoke with attended a number of different church groups, both Christians and non-Christian. The point is this: These people knew that all good gifts come from God, including their relationship and the expression of love in their relationship.

As priest, I have people come to me for marriage counseling. During these sessions I have the opportunity to hear a lot of mistaken ideas on what marriage is all about. I have heard advice that people have been given by some professional counselors that have given me a real understanding as to why some couples have gotten a divorce as the result of marriage counseling. Don't get me wrong. There are some good marriage counselors out there. However, there are some real "crackpots" with licenses to practice that have no real understanding of what makes for a God-filled, loving relationship.

Let me give you an example of what it is I am talking about: Dave and Mary were having problems in their marriage. They went to a Marriage, Family and Child Counselor (M.F.C.C. Now called a M.F.T.) in the town where they lived. One of the exercises this counselor gave Dave and Mary was to complete a "Marriage Contract." In this contract each person was to list his or her expectations of the other person. If the other person did not fulfill the listed expectations, the first person could file for divorce.

Rule number one in marriage counseling is to help the couple get out of the mode of "who's right." And to get into the mode of "what's right." Each person must look to see what they can put into the relationship, not what they can get out of the relationship.

Every couple I have worked with, and I have worked with hundreds of couples, who have put these principles to work in their relationship have recovered. They went from having a sick painful relationship where one person or the other was always leaving, to a loving, productive and joyous relationship.

You cannot hope to have a happy, loving relationship while you continue to keep one foot out the door. Either you are committed to your relationship, or you are biding time until someone else comes along. There is an old saying that relates to the topic of commitment that goes something like this: Next time you have ham and eggs for breakfast consider the different elements involved in making the meal and you will come to see that the chicken contributed to the meal, but the pig was committed.

If you want to have a healthy relationship, you cannot simply contribute to the cause. You must put all of what you have to offer into the relationship. If you do this, you will discover love.

Look to see how you can glorify God in your relationship. You cannot glorify God in your relationship while cheating on your spouse. So remain faithful in your marriage. You cannot glorify God in your relationship while you are mistreating your spouse and children. So treat them with love and kindness, and you will glorify God in your relationship. You cannot glorify God in your relationship while you lie to your spouse about things. So be truthful with your spouse and don't do things that will cause you to have to lie to your spouse.

The sole purpose for any relationship is to express love. When you express love in your relationship, you express God. We are not put here to go through life alone, but rather, to become greater expressions of God, and we do this through our relationships with other people.

Jesus said, "Inasmuch as you have done it unto the least of one of these, you have done it also unto me" (Matthew 25:40, My Translation). The things you do to your spouse you are also doing to God, for God is the living force within your spouse. You cannot say that you love God and then be abusive your spouse, for no one abuses those whom they truly love. Love never includes abuse. Remember, Jesus told us that what we do unto one another, we do also unto God.

My friend Chuck Chamberlain had one of the best definitions of love I have ever heard. He said, "If I were to define the word love in one word; that word would be action. You do things for those you love for fun and for free."

My wife is probably better at living this truth than I am. She does things all the time, not just for me, but also for many people. And she doesn't go around telling everyone about what she has done. She just quietly goes about her day helping people, and helping me to do my duties. Just as an example: As a priest I get called out at night quite often to help someone who is in crisis. Many times I will return home and find a snack waiting for me which she got out of bed to fix for me without my asking. This is just one of the things she does as an expression of her love. If I were to list everything that she does without looking for recognition, I could fill an entire book. The true expression of God here lies in the fact that she does these things for the sake of love, not ego. It has been said that, "Virtue that knows of itself is not virtue at all but ego.

Lose yourself in love and you will find yourself in God. Once you put into practice the principles we have been talking about in this chapter, you will not have to go around telling people how much you love God. Your actions will speak for themselves. I would like to leave you with the title of a song, which I think says it all. "They will know we are Christians by our love."

Notes

Chapter Sixteen

By Your Actions, Not Your Words

Have you ever met somebody who managed to work into every conversation the fact that they are a Christian? Here is one of the many experiences I have had. I had arrived at a funeral home where I was to officiate in a funeral service. Upon entering the mortuary one of the funeral home's employees walked up to me and introduced himself as John Smith (I changed his name for the sake of anonymity), a card-carrying Christian. He handed me a business card with his name on it, and under his name was the word Christian. Throughout the entire funeral service he looked up every Bible verse I used, to make sure that "Jesus really said that."

Is this what it means to be a "Christian"? My understanding of what Christianity is all about is loving God through our Lord, Jesus Christ, and loving our neighbor as ourselves.

Being a Christian is not a status symbol. It is a matter of faith, grace and love. I like how one person put it. "Live in such a way that those who know you, but don't know God, will come to know God because they know you." (Anonymous).

A good example of this came from an experience I had in the days of my youth. I came from a home that was not filled with faith. I had many questions and very little faith. I spent some time around some people who treated me with great kindness and love. They never "preached" to me or at me. They simply treated me with love and kindness. After some time had passed, I found that I wanted what they had, you know, that zest for living. I asked them what I must do in order to find in life what they themselves had found. They introduced me to their "box of spiritual tools."

If these people would have begun our relationship by bragging to me about what good Christians they were, I would have missed the message. You see I had been abused by people calling themselves Christians. My friends showed me through their actions what it means to be a Christian, and when I was moved by their great capacity to love, I asked how I could become like them.

I am reminded of a true story of a young boy who had an alcoholic father. The boy was attending a twelve-step program for children of alcoholics. This program is called Al-Ateen. I happen to be of the opinion that Al-Ateen is one of the finest programs for young people with alcoholic parents that this world has ever seen. Its principles are founded in faith, love, honesty and service to others.

While attending the meetings of Al-Ateen, this young boy learned that he was powerless over his father's drinking. He learned that he could only work on his own attitudes and actions. And that he should be loving to his father and not take it personally when his father blamed him for drinking. After all, his father would use any excuse to drink.

After being in Al-Ateen for a few months, and after working the twelve steps of that program, the boy found that his happiness and self-worth was not dependent upon his father finding sobriety.

One afternoon the boy's father had taken notice of how happy the boy was, and he wanted to know what brought about the change in his son. So he enquired about this change, asking how he could become as happy and content as his son was. Without preaching, the boy told his father about Al-Ateen, the meetings he was attending and how he had learned how to be honest with himself, and to take his focus off of his father's drinking, and concern himself with his own attitudes and actions.

The boy's father decided he wanted for himself some of what his son had found. So, the boy told his father about Alcoholics Anonymous. To this day, that boy's father has not had another drink of alcohol and many years have since passed.

What am I talking about? The principles of Christianity are very much the same. "Preaching" does very little good. If our young friend we just talked about had gone around acting "Holier than thou" with his father, he would have been viewed as a snot-nosed know-it-all kid. The same thing happens when we treat "non-believers" as though they are second-class citizens. The only one who is impressed, is the one doing the preaching.

What impressed the boy's father was the fact that the boy had changed for the better. And that is what will make people listen to us. People are impressed by the changes they see in us, not by what we preach at them. We cannot go around singing, "How great I art" and claim to be humble. It just does not work. Even Jesus said when a man referred to Him as Good Master, "Why do you call me good? There is only One who is good and that is God the Father" (Matthew 19:17, My Translation).

I have learned that of myself I can do nothing. It is only through the power of God that I am able to do the things I do. Again we are told, "For men this is impossible, but for God everything is possible" (Matthew 19:26, Lamsa Translation).

I have found that people are not impressed with my pretty words. They are moved by my loving actions. If I say I love you and I do not back up my words with actions that demonstrate love, then my words are a lie.

Action is the magic word. A wise man once said, "What you are speaks so loudly that I cannot hear what you are saying." Do your actions speak of the principles of Christianity? Or are you busy being clever with your words? I am not asking this question in order to put anyone down or to make anyone feel bad. I asked the question in the hopes that you will take a personal self-appraisal and bring your actions to match your words so you can feel good about the person you are trying to be. Or, if you are unhappy with your thoughts and actions, as well as your words, you can ask God to help you to change and grow.

Remember, it is okay to make mistakes and ask for help. This is part of practicing the principles of humility. And please remember that humility and humiliation are two different things. Being humble is not being humiliated. Being humble is to be unassuming, teachable, loving and kind.

I can remember going through a very difficult time in my life when I lost pretty much everything material in my life. I can remember thinking about all the people who said they loved me when I was on top of the world and even had a little local fame. I remember people telling me that they would stay by my side and help my family until I got back on my feet. Their words were nice, but with some of the people, it was just that. . . words. I am not saying this out of judgment. I am trying to make a point. The people who did stay by my side and call on my family, these are the ones whose actions said it all. My Bishop (H. E. Donald L. Jolly-Gabriel, Ph.D.), who is one of the most loving men I have had the joy of knowing, sent my family on a mini-vacation at his own expense to help ease their stress. That was an action of love. I had one friend who would check on me every week and bring me jokes and funny short stories to cheer me up. My point is this: these are people who are practicing the principles of Christ. They did not have to tell me how much they loved me, or that they were Christians. Their actions said it all. I know with every fiber of my being that they are the "Children of God."

Jesus said, "I was hungry, and you gave me food, I was thirsty, and you gave me drink; I was a stranger and you took me in; I was naked, and you clothed me; I was sick, and you visited me; I was in prison, and you came to me. Inasmuch as you have done it to one of the least of these my brethren, you did it to me" (Matthew 25:35-36, 40, Lamsa Translation).

I feel it necessary to restate that Christianity is not a title. It is a way of life of action based in love, faith and service to others. I am aware of members of the clergy who spend their time telling people who attend other churches that they are following the wrong faith. As far as they are concerned, the only real Christians are the one's who believe just as they do.

I also knew a wonderful Chaplain, God rest his soul (he died a few years ago in a traffic accident) who worked in a hospital, as well as for a hospice group. He served people of all faiths with love, kindness and dignity. He would go to the hospital at all hours of the day or night. He worked with cancer patients and their families. He worked with the elderly. He would visit those who were in prison. He was one of the most honest men I have ever known, and was completely selfless and humble. If you were to ask me if he was a Christian I would answer, "Yes. He is a Christian in the highest degree."

This friend I was just telling you about never went around telling people what he was doing for God's kids. He was very quiet about his actions, and would become embarrassed if you mentioned anything of his selfless labors. He was one of the happiest people I have ever known. This does not mean he never faced hard times. I watched my friend have to deal with pain and uncertainty. The way he dealt with life was by doing the footwork and leaving the results to God. He never even knew how much his income would be from month to month. He would simply go around quietly doing good deeds, and trust in God that his needs, as well as his family's needs, would be met. And you know what? His needs were always met.

Spirituality is not a theory or a philosophy. It is a way of life we must live if we are to know true joy and if we are to see the face of God. We must practice kindness, giving of what we have to those who have less than we do.

A rich man asked Jesus what it was he must do to enter the kingdom of God. Jesus told him to keep His Father's Commandments. The man said he did keep the commandments. Jesus then told him to sell all of his possessions and give the money to the poor. The man went away very sad because he equated his happiness with his possessions. His faith was in what he could see.

Jesus is not saying that we have to be dirt poor in order to get into heaven. He is telling us that we cannot afford to put anything before, or in place of our relationship with God. You see the rich man was very attached to his material wealth, and was blind to that which was behind his wealth, which is God. He could not see that God was the source of his good. So he limited what he had. He did not know that by freely giving of everything he had, he would become a clear vessel for God to fill with more of His Divinity and never-ending good.

The rich man could talk all he wanted to about how grateful he was to God for his wealth. But until he took action and shared freely of everything he had, his words were empty and meaningless. Thus, he was unable to see the kingdom of God even though he was standing in the middle of it.

Action, action, action. Demonstrate your faith as a Christian. Don't just talk about it. Don't go around telling people how loving God is. Instead, prove it to them by your loving actions. Don't preach about forgiveness. Be an example of forgiveness by forgiving people who do wrong to you. Don't talk about charity. Instead, give freely and quietly of everything you have, expecting nothing in return. Give to the poor and the homeless and don't tell anyone about your great sacrifice. Be patient with your children and understand that they are going to make mistakes. Pray to God daily in your secret place and don't take on a "Holier than thou" attitude as though you are the only one who does this. Listen to those who are in pain and don't force your solution on them. And thank God for all He is doing for you in your life, not just with your words, but by the acts of non-glorified kindness you do for all of His children of every faith, and those who have no faith whatever.

If you do these things, you will not have to tell a soul that you are a Christian. Your humble actions will sing from the mountaintops, and you will know our Father God, as expressed through our Lord, Christ Jesus. "And they will know we are Christians by our love."

Notes

Chapter Seventeen

The Prodigal Son

I want to share with you one of the most loving lessons that our Lord, Jesus tells us in the book of Luke.

"A man had two sons; and the younger son said to him, 'My father, give me my portion which is coming to me from your house.' And he divided to them his possessions. And after a few days, his youngest son gathered everything that was his share, and went to a far country, and there he wasted his wealth in extravagant living. And when all he had was gone, there was a severe famine in that country; and he began to be in need.

"So he went and got acquainted with one of the citizens of that country; and he sent him to the field to feed the swine. And he craved to fill his stomach with the husks that the swine were eating; and yet no man would give him.

"And when he came to himself, he said, 'How many hired workers are now in my father's house who have plenty of bread, and I am here perishing with hunger! I will rise and go to my father and say to him, my father, I have sinned before heaven and before you; And I am no longer worthy to be called your son; just make me like one of your hired workers.'

"And he rose up and came to his father: And while he was yet at a distance, his father saw him and had compassion on him, and he ran and he fell on his neck and kissed him. And his son said to him, 'My father, I have sinned before heaven and before you, and I am not worthy to be called your son.'

"But his father said to his servants, 'Bring the best robe and put it on him and put a ring on his hand and shoes on his feet; And bring and kill the fat ox, and let us eat and be merry; For this my son was dead and has come to life; he was lost and is found.' And they began to be merry.

"But his eldest son was in the field; and as he came near the house, he heard the voices of the singing of many. And he called one of the boys, and asked him what it was all about. He said, 'Your brother has come; and your father has killed the fat ox because he received him safe and well.'

"And he became angry and would not go in; so his father came out and besought him. But he said to his father, 'Behold, how many years have I served you, and I never disobeyed your commandment; and yet you never gave me even a kid that I might make merry with my friends. But for this son of yours, after he had wasted your wealth with harlots and come back, you have killed the fat ox.'

"His father said to him, 'My son, you are always with me, and everything which is mine is yours. It is right for us to make merry and rejoice; for this your brother was dead and has come to life; and was lost and is found.' " (Luke 15:11-32, Lamsa Translation).

This parable speaks of the depth of God's love for us as His children. It tells us of His ability and willingness to forgive us of our sins. I cannot read this beautiful lesson without weeping.

How many of us have wasted years of our lives chasing happiness in all the wrong places, until we dig ourselves into a hole that we think there can be no way out of? And then God sends to us a messenger of hope, telling us that God has not given up on us, and that He still loves us, no matter what kind of mess we have gotten ourselves into.

I want to go back and explain some of the symbols used by Jesus in this parable. They hold great meaning stemming from the Aramaic language and culture, which unfortunately gets overlooked due to the lack of understanding here in the Western world of the Eastern idioms.

When the father puts the finest robe around the son, in the Aramaic culture what he is doing is encompassing the son with his love. Wow, how powerful this is. Just think of it. Here is this boy who does everything in life wrong, who, by the opinions of our culture would be a bum. And this father, who of course represents God in this story, running out to meet him while the boy was still a ways off. And the father falls on his neck and kisses him and encompasses him in his love.

Now let's talk about the ring he puts on the son's hand. In Aramaic the ring stands for Eternal Life, it has no beginning and no end. It is whole and complete. This is what God has given to us as His children. Jesus came to show us that we are more than a body. That we are spirit and we belong to God. Jesus came and shared in our humanity, so that we may share His Divinity. He has come to put a ring upon our hand.

Next the father puts shoes on the son's feet. In Aramaic this means that the father has lifted the son from the situation he has just come from. He has raised his consciousness, if you will, to a higher level. He is on new ground. And so are we when we release the baggage we have carried in our souls, and let God love us as He heals our lives.

I am also moved by how the father comes out to be with his other son, who is so self-righteous that rather than rejoice that his brother has found life, he is angry because he wants to be the only one in heaven. Perhaps you know a few of these children of God. ...

The sad part in thinking about the self-righteous son, is the fact that he was in paradise the whole time, and did not know it. He could have killed the fat ox and made merry with his friends anytime he desired, but was blinded by his ego to the love and generosity of his father.

I hope in reading this book you have gained some insight into your soul. I pray that you will look beyond dogma and dare to search deep enough to have your very own experience with God.

I beseech you to have the courage to forgive yourself and all others who have hurt you in this life. It is only in forgiving others that we can accept God's forgiveness in our own lives.

I encourage you to do as the prodigal son did, and return to the father. It is not natural to walk through this life alone. God loves you just as you are. I cannot think of anything that any of my children could do that would ever keep me from wanting to be with them. And if I, who is a sinner, love my children this much, how much more does our Father who is perfect love us?

Don't be afraid to come home. It is the desire of God that we should know our oneness with Him. This is the message Jesus gave to us. He is our Father, and we are His Children. It is a world without end. Amen.

Made in the USA
San Bernardino, CA
11 January 2017